Don't Fight It, Just Ride It

Don't Fight It, Just Ride It

Wake-Up Call

Matt Rigsby

BEYOND BELIEF
—PUBLISHING—
YOU HOLD THE FUTURE IN YOUR HANDS

Copyright 2024 © Matt Rigsby

The author of this book does not dispense medical advice or prescribe the use of any technique as a form of treatment for physical, emotional, or medical problems without the advice of a physician, either directly or indirectly. The intent of the author is only to offer information of a general nature to help you in your quest for well-being. In the event you use any of the information in this book for yourself or others, which is your constitutional right, the author and the publisher assume no responsibility for your actions.

Statements made in this book have not been evaluated by the Food and Drug Administration. This book and its contents are not intended to diagnose, treat, or cure any infection, injury, or illness, or prevent any disease. Results vary and each person's experience is unique.

Statements made and opinions expressed in this publication are those of the author and do not necessarily reflect the views of the publisher or indicate an endorsement by the publisher.

ISBN: 978-1-957972-55-8

This book is dedicated to . . .

I dedicate this book to "Unity Consciousness" and everyone who chooses to live in an abundant, harmonious world where people are in tune with nature and treat each other with respect, regardless of our differences. Let's learn to use the gifts that we ALL have to support ourselves, our planet, and the "collective" in the best way we can.

Contents

Acknowledgments	9
Foreword	11
Introduction	13

CHAPTER ONE
   A hippie and a biker had a baby   17

CHAPTER TWO
   Who wants to be a millionaire?   25

CHAPTER THREE
   Drunks on a plane   33

CHAPTER FOUR
   The hookers and drug dealers were dancing   37

CHAPTER FIVE
   Recording studio on the beach   45

CHAPTER SIX
   The turning point   49

CHAPTER SEVEN
   Precariously perched on top of a bush   51

CHAPTER EIGHT
   Things the guidance counselor doesn't tell you   57

CHAPTER NINE
    When life gives us resistance   65

CHAPTER TEN
    Start by changing your negative thought patterns   71

CHAPTER ELEVEN
    Bridging the gap   83

About the Author   87

Acknowledgments

I would first like to thank my amazing wife Adrienne Rigsby for supporting all of my dreams, however "far out" they may seem, and allowing me the time to write. I would also like to give special thanks to Keith Leon S. for helping to reignite my passion for writing, as well as mentoring me through the writing process and my own personal growth. Last, but not least, I want to give my appreciation to Mother Earth for providing this wonderful school and playground for all of us to experience.

Foreword

As many of you know, I have been writing and publishing books for a long time now, so when my friend Matt Rigsby said he was going to write a book, I wasn't sure what to expect. I must say I was pleasantly surprised. He is an incredible writer.

In this book, Matt bares his soul and shares the stories that have transformed him into the man he is today. He has managed to illustrate the challenges that have molded him in a way that will have you on the edge of your seat, laughing at times and crying at others, with a powerful message of unity that I believe we can all learn from.

This book is a fun, easy read, written from a vulnerable place in his heart that shares the challenges and successes that have transformed him from a materialistic, corporate man into a free-spirited, well-traveled ambassador of unity consciousness that I am proud to call my friend and brother from another mother. His witty and humorous writing style manages to tackle some difficult topics with a triumphant essence that is healing and inspirational. I can't wait to read his next book.

Enjoy the read,
Keith Leon S.
Nine-Time Award-Winning, Eleven-Time International Bestselling Author; Publisher; and Award-Winning Filmmaker

Introduction

There's an old story in which an elderly man uses the story of two wolves fighting inside of us as a metaphor to illustrate inner conflict to his grandson. One wolf is good and the other one is bad. When the grandson asks, "Which one wins?" the grandfather answers, "The one we feed."

This couldn't be more true, and the stories from the *Don't Fight It, Just Ride It* series are my way of illustrating the wolves I have nurtured at different times in my life and the lessons I've learned along the way. We are all on a unique journey in this life and beyond, but we all share a consciousness we can use to do amazing things for each other and ourselves. I'm certain you will feel your vibration rising as you read these books, and this in turn raises the collective vibration, making the world a more harmonious place to live. It is my hope that reading these stories will ignite your own passions; awaken your sense of adventure, love for nature, and each other; and have a ripple effect across the planet. I've had an untraditional, some would say "crazy," adventurous life, and I plan to continue thinking and living outside of the normal boundaries that confine and stifle our vitality. Buckle up and get ready to break through your comfort zone and open up a beautiful, fulfilling life of endless possibilities without limitations!

In the nineties, I was a computer network engineer with a strong sense of adventure and love for nature, which is a bit of a paradox because computer geeks are not typically outdoorsy and adventurous, at least back then. I grew up mostly in Colorado, which is where I learned to ski and fell in love with the mountains. While a lot of people consider being on the side of a mountain during a blizzard unnecessary exposure to extreme conditions, I've always felt that it is a unique gift to be able to immerse myself in the majesty of Mother Nature while she flexes her muscles.

You see, once you get past the fact that you are alone, on the side of a mountain in a blizzard, you have no choice but to embrace her. When you do this, she embraces you back and that feeling can't be duplicated any other way. . .the high you can't buy! It gives you the clear feeling that you're not and never have been alone. This, in turn, has instilled a deep confidence, not just in me, but in the knowing the universe has my back! The following chapters will describe some amazing stories from my life and the lessons I've learned along the way. As you read, you'll notice the theme of me being a risk taker and how my "Don't Fight It, Just Ride It" approach has benefited every single aspect of my life.

Don't Fight It, Just Ride It

Embracing the blizzard in the Tetons

CHAPTER ONE

A hippie and a biker had a baby

1974 Little Matt and a random hippie

My mother was a hippie, and my daddy was a biker. He left when I was two years old because he didn't really like her (I'll spare you the rest of that song.). After returning from Vietnam, my dad was treated like a villain, the same way so many others coming home from the war were. The veterans of World War II were treated as heroes upon their return home, but most Vietnam vets had a very different reception, being called "baby killers" and worse. This caused him to reject the society that was shunning him, and he became a career biker. He wasn't the kind you see riding home from the gym with tennis shoes hanging off of the back. (Although he did tell me that hanging tennis shoes from the back seat of the Harley makes you "incognito" to the police because you look more like a yuppie than a criminal.). Rather, he was the full-on drug dealing, violent criminal variety of biker that always called his biker family a "club" rather than a "gang" because it sounded better.

To be honest, I still don't know the difference between a club and a gang, but I do remember the club doing some charitable things for the community when I was a kid, which must be what separated them from the gangs. When I was around six years old, the club hosted a Toys for Tots event, which should be a really cool thing to participate in. A convoy of Harleys carried toys to be donated to needy children for Christmas. Awesome, right?

I was riding on the gas tank of my dad's bike when we all pulled into a park and a news team came over to talk to us.

Since my dad was the president of the club, they wanted to interview him and his son—me. I was very proud my dad was doing such a good thing to help the kids and was finally getting the fame and praise he and his tattooed club brothers deserved. The nice reporter lady was asking me questions when we heard a gunshot come from across the lake. My dad and a couple of his friends instantly went into what I can only describe as "Vietnam mode" and disappeared into the trees. The rest of us took cover behind motorcycles, which is when we heard a single gunshot and then silence.

We waited a few more minutes until my dad and his friends returned to our side of the lake and the interview and festivities picked back up like nothing happened. They blamed the loud popping sound on a car backfiring and, at least from my vantage, it appeared that the disturbance was eradicated, and we could get the toys to the needy kids.

I learned many years later my dad and his friends found a lone gunman on the other side of the lake and killed him with one shot. Then some of them went back later that night and disposed of the body.

Luckily I was raised by my hippie mother, Carol, who couldn't have been more kind and loving if she wanted to. She remarried a couple of years after my dad left, to a slightly less angry Vietnam veteran, who is still my stepdad to this day. Fun fact about my mother: She has a brother named Gary, a nephew named Gary, my stepdad's name is

Gary, and my real dad's name was pronounced the same, but spelled "Gerry." What does all of this mean? As long as your name is Gary, you can pretty much treat my mom as bad as you want, and she'll keep coming back for more.

As a child of the seventies, I became part of the bridge between the industrial age and the age of information technology. My mom and stepdad both worked for Texas Instruments, which meant we always had a computer in our house from about 1980 forward. They barely resemble the computing machines of today, but ultimately they're all really just processing ones and zeros, so if you have a grasp of the original operating systems, the computers of today aren't much different at their core. If I wanted to play a game of Pong, I basically had to write a program to move the paddles up and down on the side of the screen in order to hit the ball to the other side of the screen. Little did I know I was being trained for the future.

Now, let's fast forward to 1993, when I moved to Cincinnati at twenty-one years old—partially to live closer to my dad, whom I barely knew, and partially to escape the drug-fueled, downward spiral I found myself sinking into in Texas. My plan was to spend a year or two in Cincinnati and then move back to Colorado, where I would fulfill my lifelong dream of working on ski patrol.

As a child, I vividly remember watching the people who spent their lives working in the mountains, and they had an authentic joy that wasn't common in the city. The thing that stood out the most to me was they smiled with their eyes instead of their cheeks. That spoke volumes to me about a quality of life that involves a true, deep happiness and inner peace, and it still has a strong impact on me to this day! I wanted to be one of those genuinely happy people, spending my life in nature.

After spending two years in Cincinnati getting to know my biological dad a little better, I was really glad I was raised by my mom. My father and I butted heads more often than not. No matter how hard I tried to earn his affection and respect, I only ended up disappointed. My biological dad was a violent, angry man with a smile that could warm the heart of a suicide bomber. So, I decided to pursue my ski patrol dream and leave the heart-breaking, toxic situation I was in. It was time to go skiing, or so I thought.

I took an Emergency Medical Technician (EMT) class at a local community college, and then flew to Colorado to try out for the patrol at Breckenridge, my favorite childhood mountain. The tests consisted of two days skiing every type of terrain they had to offer, with snow conditions varying from waist-deep powder to icy mogul runs and everything in between. After that, we had a day of medical testing—written and practical—and were told they would send us a letter in a couple of months to let us know if we got the job or not. The testing was in late April, so, at best, I would be starting ski patrol the following winter.

Shortly after returning to Cincinnati to wait for a job offer or rejection letter, a gal I was seeing occasionally stopped by in the middle of the day to ask if I wanted to "go to the mall, so we can talk."

Without even stepping onto the front porch, I responded, "You're pregnant, aren't you?" to which she replied, "How did you know?"

"Because I've never seen you in the daytime, and we don't really talk." It wasn't that kind of relationship. In fact, I had never met anyone from her family, and I didn't even know her last name. But that soon changed.

My introduction to her dad was uncomfortable, to say the least. "Hi. I'm the guy that knocked up your precious little girl" is a rough way to start a relationship with the future father-in-law. Nonetheless, it had to be done since she swore I was her baby daddy and I wanted to do the right thing. We decided to get married. Since I was twenty-three and she was nineteen, what could possibly go wrong?

I put my ski patrol plans on hold and bounced around from one lousy sales job to another until I finally got tired of the hustle and watching all of the profits go to those at the top, while those of us who were doing all of the heavy lifting were barely able to scrape a living together. So, I decided to take some computer classes at a community college and quickly discovered I had a knack for it and could make a significant career change for the better at a time when the Information Technology (IT) field was still in its infancy.

Midway through my first semester, I landed a job as an assistant network administrator and quit going to school shortly after because I was learning far more on the job than I ever would in that school. The school sucked pretty bad. On my last day, I stood up in the middle of class while they were showing us an infomercial on how and why to buy Cisco stock, rather than teaching us how to build computer networks, and announced all of the students taking the course should "stop wasting your money." I went on to say we weren't actually learning anything relevant to the engineering or practical skills needed to turn the course into a career, which was the goal for almost all of them.

I got bullied as a kid and have always felt a responsibility to help others when they're being taken advantage of, especially when they're making a solid effort to improve their lives. I don't know if anyone from that class listened to my warnings and quit the course, but a couple of months after I left, I got a call from another teacher from the school who heard about my not-so-subtle departure. She told me she was working on a fraud lawsuit against the school. She went on to say if I were to give a written statement about my experience, it might be helpful in getting my tuition and everyone else's reimbursed. Unfortunately, she lost the lawsuit, and I still had to pay for the "scam." This all coincided with my divorce. It was the end of a very volatile marriage that only lasted a couple of years. It is my belief a child is better off being raised by two happy parents apart, rather than two miserable parents together.

CHAPTER TWO

Who wants to be a millionaire?

By 1999, my computer career had taken off pretty rapidly, and I found myself as a high-level computer consultant, working for some very big corporations. One of these big companies is where I met Sonia, who became my second wife. She is a lovely being from Brazil. That marriage was much healthier and definitely the catalyst that got me to spread my wings and break down a lot of mental blockages getting in my way. Winning the affection of a beautiful, successful, intelligent woman did wonders for my self-confidence. Unfortunately, my ego was feeding on this like a ravenous beast.

Shortly after we started dating, I got a call from my stepmom, Mindy—which was the first time she had ever called me—to tell me my dad had just had a heart attack and died. By this time, I was twenty-seven years old and oblivious to how profoundly my father's early death would impact my future and guide me to who I would become.

Since he was a fairly healthy fifty-year-old man and both of his parents were alive and well, he apparently didn't think he was going to die anytime soon and, therefore, he hadn't prepared a will. By Ohio law, this meant his things would be divided equally among the three surviving family members of his family: me, my stepmom, and my half-brother Nick, who was eleven years old at the time. Dad didn't really have much, other than his tattoo shop and a couple of vehicles, but one of those vehicles was a very nice motorcycle that I definitely wanted.

Mindy quickly claimed I was entitled to nothing, and she never gave me so much as one of his hats.

The tattoo shop was lucrative, at least when my dad was running it, and I had no intention of pursuing any part of the business, as it was her only source of income and she had an eleven-year-old boy to raise. The only thing I wanted was his bike, more for nostalgia and sentimental reasons than anything else; I don't even remember my dad owning a car until I was about ten years old.

You see, most of my childhood memories of my dad involve me sitting on the gas tank of his chopper, cruising eighty miles an hour down some hot Texas highway with June bugs ricocheting off of my head, kinda like his windshield, and I loved it! Now that I think about it, this could explain why I love standing on top of a mountain with my face to a wind blowing so hard it makes my eyes water, then drying the tears before they roll down my cheeks. Skiing without goggles produces the same effect!

There was still some money owed on the bike, and I offered to pay it off to liberate that beautiful motorcycle from her dusty garage. Despite my best efforts, she sold the bike to a friend of hers, and I never saw it again.

More important than the bike was the welfare of my little brother, and over the next few years she would proceed to exceed my worst expectations of how things might turn out. She ran the tattoo shop into the ground and had to close permanently. She let my brother quit school at the ripe old age of fifteen. I have taken a lot of drastic measures to help him and give him a fresh start, and that, too, is a story for another book.

My father's unexpected passing at such a young age certainly made me take a good, hard look at my own life and question whether I was really making the most of it. After all, this might happen to me. When I'm preparing to leave this avatar behind, will I have a long list of things I wish I would have done? Judging by the trajectory I was on, the answer was a resounding YES! The computer work I was doing paid well, but I never felt like it was what I was meant to be doing. It wasn't fulfilling.

I decided to get out of my comfort zone and start my own consulting business. On the last day of my job working for someone else as a third-party consultant, the CEO of the company sat with me at lunch and asked, "Why are you quitting?"

I explained I was going to start my own consulting business since I was already doing all of the work. This would allow me to charge less money than the current consulting company, and I would take home a lot more than I was at that time.

He caught me off guard by asking, "Would you like to come out to my dressage farm and discuss what could be your first project as an independent contractor?"

The universe loves to see us take action and always rewards us for paying attention when she nudges us to go in a particular direction and we follow her guidance. Of course, I said "yes" as I tried to control my enthusiasm and soon learned what the expression "more money than God" meant.

John was quite a presence. He told me he had patented barcodes in the 1950s—not invented, but patented, nonetheless. He also told me he had designed and patented a camera that could judge the surface density of outer planetary objects, and he was instrumental in finding a landing spot on the moon for the Apollo spacecraft. During John's early years, he was a proud member of the Navy Special Forces and was asked to be one of the original Navy Sea, Air, and Land Teams (SEAL) instructors, which he declined because he wanted to go to college on the G.I. bill and become an engineer.

When I arrived at John's office at the dressage farm—dressage is a sport; a rider sits atop a very expensive horse that has been trained to do the moonwalk and ballet-type movements—the first things I noticed were all of the pictures of him taken with current and past U.S. presidents, on the wall behind his desk. As I sat down across from him, he handed me a piece of paper, with a slight chuckle, and said, "What do you think I ought to do about this?"

I proceeded to read a simply written paragraph asking him to be the Secretary of the U.S. Navy, signed by none other than Donald Rumsfeld, the Secretary of Defense! I put the letter back on his desk and said, "I bet you'll make a lot more money and have a lot less stress if you just keep doing what you're doing."

He replied, "I knew I liked you, and that's exactly what I'm going to do." And so began my friendship with the "financially" wealthiest man I've ever known.

The project he hired me to do was incredibly complicated, and it led me to getting a patent in 1999 on a system that utilized wireless technology when wireless was in its infancy. John was quite pleased that I managed to pull it off with a pretty tight time restriction and told me he was going to make me a millionaire. I would do the engineering and documentation, while he funded future projects, and we would split the profits 50/50.

As I got to know his family and his so-called friends, I began to question whether I wanted to be a millionaire at all. None of his relationships appeared to be genuine or authentic because everyone was constantly kissing his ass, and he knew it! I could tell he didn't like it and couldn't change it, either, at least not without getting rid of all of his money and seeing who was still at his side, so I made it a point to be the opposite toward him. Even his own kids were stealing from him on a regular basis, which I know because they became friends of mine. . . at least until I got the full picture of what type of people they really were. He commented several times on how much he appreciated my "candor and authenticity."

If hearing things about 9/11 triggers you, you may want to move ahead to the next chapter.

Business was going great, and it looked like my first contract was about to lead into a lucrative career. Feeling comfortable enough, Sonia and I decided to buy a nice house in the country, just outside of Cincinnati. I was checking all of the boxes:

- Lots of time with my son
- Great wife
- Nice cars
- Nice house
- Business is good
- Traveling a lot

The house was much nicer than my twenty-year-old self would have ever imagined I could own. The five-and-a-half-acre yard looked like a state park and had a class-4 creek running through the backyard, which soon became my favorite place on Earth!

Shortly before we moved to this Shangri La in the country, 9/11 happened, and my friend/business partner disappeared for six months, causing me to shift gears and take on new endeavors to pay the bills.

After resurfacing six months later, John told me he "checked himself into a mental hospital," which was where he had been all of that time. He said he lost about 70 million dollars on 9/11, but that's not what "drove him off the deep end." Instead, he had a mental breakdown because of what happened when he was at the airport in Houston on the tenth of September, about to board a plane to go to New York to attend a meeting at the Twin Towers. He received a phone call from someone powerful—he never told me who it was or exactly what was said—and was advised not to go to New York and not to be in the Twin Towers.

This meant someone knew what was going to happen and did nothing to stop it. So he did what any good-hearted man would do in this situation and lost his fucking mind.

This was the proverbial straw that broke the camel's back for me, at least as far as pursuing riches in the corporate world. Part of me wishes John had never told me about the phone call because it completely unraveled the very foundation of everything I was raised to believe—that the government is chosen by us and will protect us.

I'm not going to dive too deep into this tragedy that altered the lives of every single American and most of the world, except to say the government knew when and where the attack was going to happen, which is really all I know about it anyway.

Stay with me folks; I promise it's about to get fun!

CHAPTER THREE

Drunks on a plane

By the spring of 2006, my good friend Jimmy returned from Iraq after working as a civilian contractor during the Gulf War. As a beneficiary of the military-industrial complex, he made a small fortune installing motion sensors on military vehicles, and he was certain he'd blow it all on his alcoholic tendencies and the problems that come with that. We were both in our early thirties, and back then I loved to party. I didn't really have a drug of choice, but I liked most of them. Looking back, I realize I used them partially to feed my hunger for adventure and new experiences, but also to avoid dealing with reality.

Let's not forget my mother was a hippie and my daddy was a biker, so drugs were always around when I was growing up. I can't even remember whether I tried acid (LSD) or weed first. Either way, I was a ripe fourteen years old when I started that stuff.

Jimmy, on the other hand, liked to get drunk and pass out two or three times a day. When he was sober-ish and coherent, he was absolutely hilarious and a lot of fun to be around.

Shortly after his return, we met up for a couple of cocktails to catch up on the two years he was gone, and that day turned into *way* more than either of us expected.

We proceeded to drink like we were going to the electric chair as he told me about his alcoholic concerns. Me being a "helper" by nature, I started trying to figure out what kind of life would make Jimmy happy and help him avoid the tragic life of a down-and-out alcoholic. I asked him, "What's your favorite thing on Earth to do?"

He promptly replied, "I just wanna go fishing every day!"

I went on to tell him about my experience fishing off the Pacific coast of Costa Rica and how the sailfish and marlin are practically jumping in the boat. Back then, Costa Rica used to cost a lot less to live in than the U.S., and he had more than enough money to buy a boat and a house and start a fishing business of his own. He explained that he wasn't comfortable going to a foreign country alone and asked if I would go with him sometime.

I said that I would love to go fishing with him in Costa Rica "sometime."

Twelve hours later, I was rudely awakened by the sound of a stewardess telling me that I needed to fill out some immigration paperwork. The fog in my head was thick and I felt like I might be dreaming—until I looked over and saw Jimmy passed out in the seat next to me. I immediately asked the nice lady, "Where are we going and aren't you supposed to stop drunk people from getting onto airplanes?"

She replied, "We are about thirty minutes from landing in San Jose, Costa Rica, and we're well past the point of no return."

Panic set in when I remembered my wife was out of the country and I had two dogs and two cats to take care of. Upon landing, I immediately went to the ticket counter to get on the next flight home, only to be told there were no available flights back to Cincinnati for ten more days.

My panic turned into full-on freaking out. I called Jack, my next-door neighbor, and began to explain the predicament I had gotten myself into. I told him where the spare key was and asked if he could please take care of my critters and keep an eye on the house while I was gone.

He started laughing hysterically, which I thought was pretty heartless, then went on to tell me, "You came over here last night and gave me the key and the instructions for the animals."

My relief was quickly overshadowed by the fact I still had to call Sonia to explain why I was stuck in Costa Rica for ten days. As you can imagine, that conversation went over like a turd in the punch bowl, and I'm sure to this day she still doesn't believe I was actually stuck there.

Once I accepted the reality of my situation, I took a look inside my duffel bag to see what I had packed in my drunken stupor. There were two pairs of swim trunks, a couple of tank tops, and some bongos (a pair of small drums). Luckily that was exactly what I needed for this particular trip.

CHAPTER FOUR

The hookers and drug dealers were dancing

We caught a taxi to go visit a local friend of mine named Diego, who is a world-class whitewater kayaker and a fitting ambassador for Costa Rica. He's the same age as me, and he's a tad bit crazy with a heart of gold! Costa Rican culture is a lot less hung up on morality than the U.S., which is not to say they are immoral; only that they are very open and accepting of things we might call taboo. This makes them easy to get along with, and they definitely embody the Don't Fight It, Just Ride It mentality.

Upon our arrival, Diego and two other guys were packing a bunch of kayaks and gear into his van to take to the ocean, and he strongly recommended we join them. The plan was to take whitewater kayaks called "play boats," which are designed to surf and do tricks like cartwheels and flips in rivers, to the ocean and see what kind of fun we could turn that into. We jumped in the van and headed to Jaco, a cozy little surf town on the Pacific coast. In 2006, Jaco was a quiet town with a seedy underbelly. There were a few small restaurants and bars along the beach and a main strip, which is where most of the action was after the sun went down. The waves there are big, glassy, and consistent—absolutely perfect for surfing, and it was a good place for us to book a deep-sea fishing trip.

The next morning came with a pretty good hangover, but it was overshadowed by our excitement to try something new. None of the folks in our posse had ever surfed ocean waves in a kayak before, so it would be a first for all of us, except Jimmy. Jimmy decided to take on the noble task of trying to rid the world of alcohol by drinking it all, and his dedication to his mission was tenacious, to say the least. After grabbing some breakfast, we headed to the black sand Pacific beach.

We got in our kayaks and paddled out to where there were already a dozen or so people on surfboards catching perfect waves. Local surfers can be a little (extremely) territorial. A few of them struck up conversations with us, curious why we were in whitewater kayaks. I sort of expected them to tell us to get off their wave. Instead, they were stoked and welcoming (Don't Fight It, Just Ride It).

In Costa Rica, they like to say *Pura Vida*, which means "pure life," and we were embodying that as far as they were concerned. We explained we weren't sure what was going to happen, but we were about to find out!

Three out of the four of us caught a wave at the same time, and I instantly felt at one with the wave! I've surfed standing up in the ocean, and I've surfed kayaks in rivers, but this was different. Using a paddle to catch a wave took about as much effort as sending a kite up in a strong wind—not hard at all. The shape of the boat made carving turns and doing cartwheels on the face of the wave surprisingly easy and magical in a way I never could have imagined. When we started, the waves were about nine feet overhead with barrels that looked like a rolling portal to another dimension. It was absolutely pure bliss gliding the glassy waves with such ease and control! Everyone in the crew was better than average at river kayaking, which translated beautifully onto the ocean. It was definitely one of the best days I've ever spent in a kayak, and I've spent a lot of days in a kayak!

With the boat at a right angle, we were able to throw so many cartwheels, it would make us dizzy and a little nauseous. Other times we would ride the wave into the tube, which was a perfect blue tunnel, enclosing all around us except for the blue light at the end. Sometimes we'd make it to the end of the tube just in time to feel the blast on our backs from the massive wave collapsing onto itself. At other times we'd get pounded by the waves landing on top of us, at which point we would be "rag-dolled" around in the surf, and that was pretty fun too!

We decided to take a break after a couple of hours to grab some food and were greeted by a bunch of onlookers who were just as stoked as we were about what just went down. Even the hardcore local "standup" surfers were giving us high fives and buying us beers.

We found Jimmy diligently carrying out his mission to rid the world of alcohol at the bar sitting next to a famous musician. I greeted the guy and said, "Hey, aren't you so and so? I like your music."

He coldly replied, "Yeah, that's nice." He seemed to have a problem talking to a mere peasant like me, so I admitted I didn't really like his music and I was just trying to be nice.

We ended up doing some shots and got too drunk to go back to the ocean, so we continued to party until the moon told us to go to bed. The next morning, Diego directed me to a friend of his who owned a fishing boat, in hopes that we could book a trip. After that, we made plans to meet up again before I headed back to the States.

Just about the time I started to think the highlight of the trip was over, I met an eighteen-year-old blonde-haired, blue-eyed, bushy-tailed fella from Florida named Jason, carrying a guitar on his back. Jason explained he had "recently inherited enough money to never have to work a day in my life." He was radiating the aura of a jolly old soul and said he was going to travel the world without ever getting on a plane. Instead, he wanted to go by bus, boat, bicycle, train, or car, not because he was afraid of flying, but because he wanted to take his time to get to know the people and places a little better and take the time to really get a feel for the flavor of the cultures all over the globe. Jason was wise beyond his years.

I have always believed we *must* travel a lot to have an accurate worldview. Otherwise, you're relying on stories from other people that are usually not accurate and which are influenced by their opinions, rather than facts.

We talked about music, and he said, "Playing music comes very naturally to me, but songwriting seems impossible." I told him about my process for writing songs and poems, and then we headed to my hotel room to get my songbook so I could show him what I was talking about. I had about forty songs in a notebook, which I tore five pages from and gave to him in hopes he could use them as a tool to start writing songs himself.

He saw my bongos in the corner and suggested we go outside and play some music together. We walked down to the main strip, found a good spot to sit on the sidewalk, and began playing some absolutely fantastic music. Jason was a much better guitar player than I was a drummer, but luckily he knew how to dumb it down so I could be included.

After a few minutes, someone asked, "Where's your tip jar?" This hadn't crossed our minds, so Jason opened up his guitar case, and it quickly filled up with cash. Before long, there were a lot of people dancing on the sidewalk and it totally changed the seedy dynamic of that surf town, at least for a little while. There were hookers and drug dealers dancing and giving us money, instead of trying to hustle everyone.

About an hour into our jam session, a man got my attention to tell me, "If you really want to know why you brought your instruments to Costa Rica, meet me on the beach in thirty minutes, and you will understand."

More than a little curious, we decided to follow his instructions. I started counting the money to split with Jason, who really deserved all of it, when he stopped me and said, "Keep it all. I already have enough money." That certainly was not the kind of thing I was accustomed to hearing rich people say, so I kept all but one unique gold coin, which I gave to him as a reminder of the first time he played music on the street with some random guy he'd just met and how magical it was.

We packed up and went to the firepit on the beach, as directed by the mysterious stranger, to find the beach dark, quiet, and empty, with the exception of a massive full moon, perched perfectly on the horizon. It seemed to be melting into the ocean as the waves pulled the light toward us. Absolutely breathtaking. With full-body goosebumps, we played to the moon for about fifteen minutes until the mystery man and nine of his jovial friends showed up dressed in all black.

They were professional fire dancers touring Central and South America, and they wanted to practice on the beach while we played music. They started a bonfire, which they used to ignite their various juggling gadgets. Some of them were twirling flaming batons. Some of them were throwing chains spinning into the air with flaming balls on each end. One guy even lit a sword on fire and swallowed it! Definitely not what I thought I was going to be doing with my bongos when I pulled them out of my duffel bag at the airport.

With at least thirty people dancing around the firepit, it didn't take long for a crowd to build. All four elements were showing off in one of the most spectacular displays I've ever witnessed, much less been a part of. The sound of the waves breaking onto the beach began keeping time as we played, and the entire scene was almost enough to make my heart explode with universal love. I looked at Jason, and we both had tears running down our cheeks while smiling so big I can still feel it to this day. We played until my hands were sore and swollen and we were completely exhausted.

That wraps up one of the best nights I've ever had. Jason, if you're still out there, I'm still waiting to hear one of those songs I gave you on the radio.

I got back to the room to find Jimmy catching up on his beauty sleep, but I had to wake him up and tell him what he had missed. He grumbled some inarticulate drunken slur and went back to trying to make himself prettier. The following night would prove to be no less interesting.

CHAPTER FIVE

Recording studio on the beach

After breakfast, Jimmy and I decided to set up a fishing trip and rent some surfboards for the day, but it was a blazing hot day, so we spent more time inside at the bar than we did on the beach. Again, Jimmy went to sleep shortly after sundown, so I decided to go outside and write some songs on the beach.

I found a nice piece of driftwood, where I set up my own little recording studio with my bongos and a pocket recorder. A pocket recorder is a device that has a small cassette tape in it for recording purposes. The one I had would hold about two hours on each side of the cassette. I was playing to another full moon melting into the ocean for an hour or so with my headphones on, totally in "the zone," when a man about ten years older than me tapped me on the shoulder and scared the shit out of me.

He told me he noticed me playing music, and he wanted me to have his guitar, which was in his apartment nearby. He said his name was Kevin, and I could have everything in his apartment. I thought this mighty generous and asked him what he planned to do.

Kevin replied, "I came here twenty years ago on vacation from Canada with a heroin addiction, and when I got here I found out I could get liquid morphine from the pharmacy with no questions asked, so I never left. I've been here shooting up morphine for the last twenty years, and I can't live like this anymore. So I quit, cold turkey, five days ago. I can't live like this either, so I'm going to swim to Hawaii."

This was an ambitious goal, to say the least. I suggested he show me this apartment he was leaving behind, and we could bring his guitar down to the beach and play a few songs together before he took the big swim. Kevin thought it was a good idea, so we ventured back to his apartment, got his guitar, and headed back to my recording studio on the beach. Our music was a far cry from the magic that happened the night before, but the withdrawals he was suffering from probably had a lot to do with it.

We played and told stories until the sun came up, at which point I said, "I'm sorry to leave you, but I have to get some sleep." He agreed sleep was a good idea, so we hugged and cried as we said our goodbyes, and he insisted the universe put me there so he wouldn't end his own life.

At the time, I thought it was just a coincidence I was there, but now I know Kevin was right. It was uncharacteristic of me to just take off to another country without any preparation at all. Especially while Sonia was out of the country and I had critters to take care of, but the universe truly does work in mysterious ways. I know now that there are no coincidences, but there is divine intervention, which in this case benefited Kevin. The bongos were the key to starting all of those interactions. AMAZING! Don't Fight It, Just Ride It!

After napping for a couple of hours, I woke up and realized I had left my pocket recorder on that piece of driftwood, so I jumped out of bed and ran out to retrieve it, only to find the beach was full of people and the pocket recorder was gone. There were a couple of years' worth of songs, poems, and random thoughts on that gadget, which definitely meant a lot more to me than whoever ended up with it. In fact, it stifled my desire to write for a long time, but helping Kevin in such a big way made it a lot easier to stomach.

Jimmy and I scheduled a couple of different fishing trips, but never made it to any of them. My pickled buddy's chronic routine of getting hammered every day made it impossible for him to get up early enough to go fishing. That definitely reinforces the divine intervention theory, as we were obviously not there for Jimmy to figure out how to start a fishing business. We spent the rest of the trip partying from town to town.

This remains one of the most influential experiences of my life and still shapes how I view life and carry myself to this day. When I got off that plane, my first thought was I had just screwed up royally and needed to fix it right away. Now, with the benefit of hindsight, I know that's exactly where I was supposed to be and what I was supposed to be doing, from a universal perspective. I got drunk and traveled 3500 miles to intervene in Kevin's suicide. My wife didn't share my enthusiasm for this serendipitous miracle that saved Kevin, and this incident was definitely one of the contributing factors to our divorce later that year.

I haven't talked to Kevin since then, and I truthfully don't even remember his real name, but a character in a story needs a name, and I feel like he was a "Kevin." At any rate, he was and is a real person and if you're that guy and reading this, please look me up. I'd love to hear how your life's been since the universe brought us together!

CHAPTER SIX

The turning point

By the time 2006 came around, I was super stressed over a corrupt business partner and some other life events that had me feeling smothered by what my life was becoming, and my marriage was on the rocks because of it. As a last-ditch effort to save my eroding marriage, I suggested we sell everything, move to the mountains of West Virginia, and start fresh. Sonia declined, and we decided to part company. We had been growing apart for a while, and it was obvious we had very different long-term goals. I wasn't exactly sure what my long-term goal was at the time, but I knew it wasn't sitting in traffic every day, driving to a job I didn't love, just for the sake of making a paycheck so I could buy more crap I didn't need until I had so much crap I would need a bigger house to put it all in.

Sonia had grown up poor in Brazil and worked her butt off to get herself out of poverty and became a chemical engineer for a big corporation, so the money was a lot more important to her than it was to me. She could afford the house payments without me, so I signed it over to her and gave her everything that didn't fit in my truck. I felt guilty for not trying harder to make the marriage work, since she had moved all the way from Brazil to marry me, but she did become a U.S. citizen out of the deal and remarried about a year after our divorce, so that definitely helped my conscience.

It came with a heavy heart and a lot of second-guessing, but I was finally on my way to live in the mountains and fulfill the ski patrol dream I had put on hold twelve years earlier. My son's mom agreed to alternate school years with me, and the idea was that Zack would spend a school year with her, as I got settled in West Virginia, and the next year he would be with me. It was only four hours away, and we planned to meet and do the kid swap as much as possible.

Long story short—she never let him spend a school year with me, so I became more of a "Disneyland" dad at that point, seeing him during the summer and a few times during the school year. For years I held onto a grudge toward her about this. But truth be told, I was a pretty big, self-absorbed mess for a couple of years after the divorce—not exactly role model material—so the universe did what was best because I still had some big lessons to learn. On the upside, Zack had some amazing experiences when he visited that never would have happened had I remained tame and domesticated.

CHAPTER SEVEN

Precariously perched on top of a bush

With Adrienne Rigsby and her sister Carly below Sweets Falls on the Gauley River

After my first season of ski patrolling at Snowshoe Mountain ended, I moved to a tent in the woods at a rafting company in Fayetteville, West Virginia, and things got silly. I originally thought a job on the river would be a fun way to kill time between ski seasons, but it turned into way more than just something I did until the next ski season started, and boating became a much bigger part of my life than skiing.

I only lived in the tent for about a month before I moved into a house (self-preservation is important), but I saw more crazy shit in that month than I had seen in the ten years prior. This particular outfit boasted more off-river deaths than any other company around, and in West Virginia that's oddly competitive.

On a scale of 1 to 10, the party scene was an 11, which occasionally led to some folks becoming un-alived in one fashion or another. I never witnessed any of that, but I heard plenty of stories of people getting shot or stabbed or overdosing, and lots of other wholesome activities that are fun for the whole family. I did have a dear friend from Costa Rica named David who was stabbed multiple times by some tweaker from a different rafting company. He got life-flighted to the hospital, where he almost died a couple of times. Luckily, he was too strong and stubborn to die and is still alive and well in Costa Rica. In fact, if you find yourself in Costa Rica, you should look him up at his business, Sarapiqui Outdoor Center. I'm sure he would love to take you rafting!

One night a drunk-ass raft guide named Craig thought it would be fun to light the loose fringe hanging off the back of one of the guests' cut-off blue jean shorts on fire. They went up in flames pretty quickly. Craig was kind enough to apologize and repeatedly slap the guest on the ass until the fire went out. By this time the guy was justifiably pissed off and told Craig to go fuck himself, and then he headed to the bathroom to address his wounds.

Craig felt like the guy didn't receive his apology appropriately and followed him to the bathroom where he proceeded to smash a beer bottle over the guy's head. I guess Craig needed to reinforce his sincerity. For this indiscretion with a customer, he was suspended for a week from work. This was the culture I fell into. As a side note, that week's suspension didn't curb Craig's craziness at all.

Beyond all of the chaos, there was far more beauty and some truly amazing souls I got to know that summer, one of them Safari Charlie. Charlie, who has since passed on, was in the upper echelon of alcohol enthusiasts, which definitely led to his early demise. He earned the nickname "Safari" Charlie because most mornings he usually crawled out of the woods at the rafting company, either drinking a beer or trying to find one. He also had some serious "living drunk in the woods" skills. I never saw him getting out of a tent. He would make himself a bed by weaving the branches of a rhododendron bush together in a way that is pretty comfortable when it's done right, and downright dangerous when it's done wrong.

It's difficult to overstate how shocking it is to wake up from a drunken stupor by slamming your head and neck against the ground as your knees crash down into your face, knocking the wind out of you, while the thick branches from your "bush bed" are jabbing into your possibly broken ribs. You are then hit with the realization you need to either poop or throw up, but your feet are still tangled above your head. All this before you need to go to work on the river. The moral of the story is to take your time and weave your bed *right* and *do not* try rolling over in your sleep when you're perched on top of a bush, on the side of a mountain. Rest in peace, brother Charlie!

I did the ski bum and raft guide cycle on repeat for a few years, until one summer I decided to throw being a zipline guide into the mix. The zipline course was brand new, and my rock-climbing experience gave me enough familiarity with the harnesses and equipment to get a job as one of the first zipline guides in West Virginia. I even got interviewed by and gave a tour to some reporters from *Popular Mechanics* magazine who quoted me by name for an article they did on the course in 2009 (my big claim to fame).

Being a zipline guide is also how I met my current and favorite wife, Adrienne. A fitting introduction because she loves monkeys so much. It's fun to tell people we met on the top of a tree in West Virginia, but the truth is we met on the ground first—although we definitely connected as soon as we were flying through the treetops together, 100 feet off the ground.

The surfboard had to make my 86 VW Cabriolet more aerodynamic.

CHAPTER EIGHT

Things the guidance counselor doesn't tell you

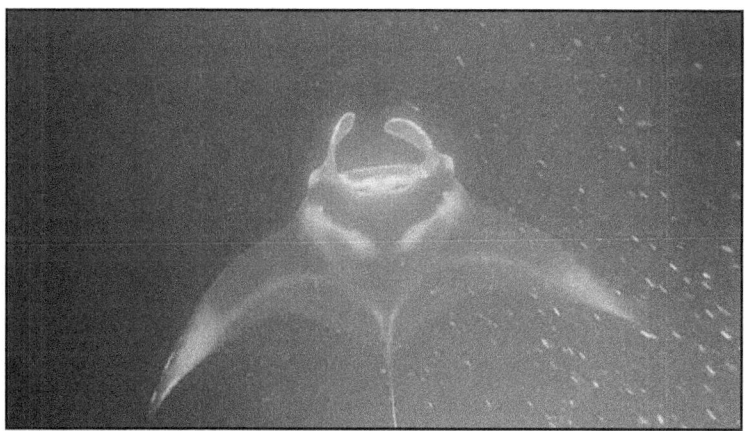

Giant manta ray off the coast of Kona, Hawaii

When I moved to West Virginia, I knew I would be spending my summers working on the river, but I wasn't sure whether I'd be "video" kayaking or guiding rafts. A video kayaker is someone who kayaks along with the rafting trip and shoots video of the rafts going through the rapids and surfing, in the hope customers will buy the video at the end of the day. It didn't pay much, but you get a ride to the river, a free lunch, and a ride back to town after having a blast kayaking down amazing rivers alone. (Kayaking class 5 whitewater alone is not recommended, in case you're wondering.).

I had a lot of experience in a kayak and pretty much zero in a raft. But I did know raft guides got paid a lot more per trip and got tips, with the added benefit of meeting lots of women on vacation in "Wild and Wonderful" West Virginia. As a freshly bachelorized man, I can honestly say the latter of reasons given above was ultimately what solidified my decision to be a raft guide. What I didn't know was how profound an impact taking a bunch of strangers class 5 rafting would have on my life.

Most of the rafters were totally out of their element and ranged from being a little bit nervous to downright terrified before every trip. As a guide, a big part of the job is to comfort them and try to instill some confidence. People have a lot more fun and embrace the moment much more easily when they're not scared out of their minds. A little fear is a good thing, but being riveted by it is not. Witnessing the transformation of a whole bunch of people when they go from "Holy shit! What have I gotten myself into? We're all gonna die!" to "This is the most amazing day of my life!" is definitely one of my favorite ways to spend the summers. I've formed stronger bonds with some folks in five or six hours on a river than I have in a lifetime with most of my family members. In fact, I liked it so much, I now own a rafting company in Salmon,

Idaho, on the Salmon River called Kookaburra. Look me up if you're in the area, and I'd be honored to share my love for the river with you someday, too!

West Virginia is loaded with stunning natural beauty and is home to some of the best whitewater on the planet! Once a raft guide adds the Upper Gauley (big class 5+ river) to their resume, they can get guide work pretty much anywhere on Earth. I put that theory to the test, and for the next six years I guided on rivers all over this country and several others.

Pay attention, kids. I'm going to tell you all you need to do to succeed anywhere on this planet in almost any job that doesn't require a doctorate:

- Be on time consistently.
- Be eager to learn.
- Have integrity. Do the right thing, even when you think nobody is watching.

That's it! Do these three things, and someone with seniority in whatever field you've chosen to pursue will see you're taking initiative and show you the ropes to ensure you succeed. It's really that simple. Doing the least amount possible seems to be trending these days, which will make it even easier for anyone with a decent work ethic to get ahead. If what you're doing currently doesn't feel right in your bones, keep trying new things until you find something that does. That feeling is the universe's way of trying to keep you pointed in the right direction.

The right direction leads you to a life that is fulfilling and brings you the most joy, and that is different for each of us. Listen to the little voice in your head telling you to get out of your comfort zone and try something bold and new. Don't you want to live your best life possible?

As I traveled from river to river, I started to see a lot of the same faces, even on the other side of the planet. There's a small, but growing, subculture of river folk spanning the globe, and they are some of the most solid human beings I know—not counting the fugitives, of course. Most of them are doers rather than talkers and are far more interested in authentic experiences and relationships than materialism. There are a lot of highly educated river chauffeurs out there sporting unused college degrees from just about every field you can think of.

The Don't Fight It, Just Ride It lifestyle took me to a lot of unexpected places with some amazing jobs that my high school guidance counselor never mentioned. The one that stands out as my favorite, without question, was guiding night dives with giant manta rays off of the coast of Kona, Hawaii.

In the summer of 2011, Adrienne and I moved to Hawaii and stayed with Kris and Eric, some of Adrienne's friends from her days as a zookeeper in Indiana. We got jobs as sea kayak guides and, shortly after starting, the owner of the company asked us if we wanted to try swimming with giant manta rays that night—a no brainer, right? We showed up at sunset and kayaked out about a half mile, got in the water, and waited as the sun disappeared into the ocean. The method for attracting mantas was an experiment involving a surfboard with a big hole bored through the center of it with some super bright LED lights shining through the surfboard, down into the dark abyss. The hope was that the lights would attract plankton, which would then attract mantas. It worked *way* better than any of us expected!

As the six of us floated on the surface, looking into the water with a snorkel and a mask, three of the biggest, most elegantly graceful creatures I've ever seen came out of the darkness and began feeding on the plankton our lights had attracted. The largest of them had an eighteen-foot wingspan and a mouth that could swallow a person whole, yet I felt very comfortable swimming in the middle of the Pacific Ocean with them.

Even though there were six of us in the water, the mantas took a particular liking to me. They proceeded to do big, sweeping barrel rolls and, each time they circled back to the ocean's surface, they would rub their bellies against mine as they swam under me, which would gently lift me out of the water and then gently set me back down. I could clearly feel we had a connection, and it's something everyone should experience at least once!

After being surrounded by the mantas for about half an hour, I started to feel a little awkward from all of the attention I was getting, and it didn't appear to be letting up anytime soon. The owner of the company asked if any of us wanted to guide trips like this, to which we all said YES! He looked at me and said, "They picked you, Matt." After that, I started going out to play with the docile sea creatures five or six nights a week.

My days consisted of taking people sea kayaking in the morning, and we'd do some snorkeling and cliff jumping while we were out, usually returning around one o'clock in the afternoon. Then I'd usually grab some food and go surfing or paddle boarding in the afternoon until it was time to go back to work just before sunset. From our shop on the beach, we would hop in our kayaks—mine towing the surfboard with the lights—and paddle out into the Pacific to find a mooring ball I would use to tie all of the boats. Everyone would get in the water and hold onto the rope that went around the surfboard. With their bodies lying flat on the surface and their faces looking into the water, I would tow them and the surfboard around until the mantas showed up.

Even without the mantas, kayaking into the Pacific at sunset is an experience I will never forget. On a clear day, way out in the ocean at sunset, there's a thing called the "green flash" that happens when the sun shines through all the water curving around the Earth, but only for a fraction of a second, so trying to see it can be a little bit like catching lightning in a bottle. The conditions have to be just right, but I was lucky enough to experience a whole bunch of them while kayaking out to visit with the mantas.

There were a lot of nights mantas wouldn't show up for the guests, so I would jump in the water. For some reason, they would always make an appearance. Sometimes it would only be long enough for them to say hi and leave, but they made an appearance, nonetheless.

Every now and then a big shark would swim through the light, but they never seemed too interested in what we were doing. As the guide, part of my job was to comfort the guests while they were in the water, which is not easy to do when a fourteen-foot tiger shark enters the frame. In fact, a lot of nights were downright spooky. While paddling back to shore, we were frequently floating through water glowing green with bioluminescent plankton. Thousands of sardine-sized fish would jump several feet out of the water! Sometimes they would smack us right in the face. By the time we reached shore, there would be dozens of the festive little critters flopping all over the inside of the kayak. We saw a lot of flying fish, too, but none of them bounced off of my head.

CHAPTER NINE

When life gives us resistance

Our amazing Hawaiian summer came to an end, and we ventured to Costa Rica for a month to go rafting and exploring with David, my friend who owns Sarapiqui Outdoor Center. We had no real agenda and unwittingly became part of their Independence Day celebration.

Costa Rican people used to be ruled by a harsh dictator, and the story we were told is that to get out from under his tyranny, they burnt his house to the ground at four in the morning on September 15th, 1821, with him in it, which is why the official party starts at four in the morning. Some folks commemorate this by making paper houses and burning them. The unofficial party starts the night before because it's much easier to stay awake partying all night than it is to get motivated to celebrate anything at four in the morning.

As you can imagine, things get pretty silly after you've been pre-partying until four a.m. Then things kick into high gear. I won't elaborate more than that, except to say Ticos—local Costa Ricans—know how to throw a serious party, and they celebrate their independence with more vigor and joy than anyone, anywhere else I've ever seen. There were a whole bunch of awesome adventures packed into that month, and you can read about those in my next book.

The reason I've been telling you these stories is to paint a picture of the events that have shaped me and my views on life thus far. As you may have noticed, I tend to go with the flow, and Don't Fight It, Just Ride It means a lot more than that to me. It works as a good overall philosophy for life, and it's a very useful approach to life's many challenges. I've learned that when life gives us resistance, it's best not to react with more resistance. In fact, it's best not to react at all. But this is easier said than done.

It's important to be patient with all situations and let things unfold as the universe sees fit. When we react immediately to conflict, we usually just create more conflict. Where your thoughts go, energy flows. Focus your thoughts on an outcome that benefits everyone, when possible, and I promise life will get easier for you and those close to you. It's also crucial that we stop taking ourselves so seriously! Life is meant to be fun, so be silly and stop worrying about what other people think.

After leaving Costa Rica, Adrienne and I bounced between West Virginia, Colorado, Utah, and Idaho for another two years. We settled in Idaho, which we will always call home, at least when we're not living on a sailboat. I'm reluctant to say much about Idaho, because we want it to stay like it is, but I will say the potatoes are cheap here! There are no jobs, the internet service is slow as molasses, and the real estate is outrageously overpriced, but it's a great place for you to visit for a couple of weeks and then go back home.

The last fifty-one years have been loaded with successes and failures, but I have managed to re-create those deep wrinkles on the sides of my eyes I recognized on the happy mountain elders' faces when I was a kid skiing in Colorado. I firmly believe we have to leave our comfort zones to grow as humans, and we should frequently check in with ourselves to make sure we're not getting too comfortable for too long.

In the eighteen years since leaving the corporate world and city life behind, I've had just about every job possible at ski resorts across the country, and I have managed to ski a lot more days than your average billionaire. So take that, corporate America! I've also found a way to be on or in the water almost every summer, and I now own a rafting company. One thing I haven't mentioned yet, in this book, is that I absolutely love sailing and have dreamt for a couple of decades of sailing around the world. Now I'm at a stage in my life where it's time to break *way* out of my comfort zone again.

I was planning to sell the rafting company last summer and move onto a sailboat to begin my journey around this rock hurtling through space that we live on. But the universe had other plans. Instead, the universe has inspired me to pass on the experience and knowledge I've gained over the years to the younger generation before I disappear into the wild blue yonder! One of the most important lessons I've learned is when the universe nudges you to do something, *you better do it*, or the nudges become pushes, and then comes the body slam!

Again, I implore you to trust your intuition and go with the feeling in your gut—that is the universe guiding you to make choices which will benefit you at some point. It's not always obvious what the long-term benefit will be, but if you fight your intuition, you will never find out what magic the universe has in store for you!

If something doesn't feel right and good, you should keep trying new things until you land on something that is fulfilling emotionally. I also want to stress the importance of feeling your emotions. We often push the bad ones as deep as we can because they're unpleasant to feel and think about. If you do this long enough, your emotions will accumulate in your body in the form of some type of dis-ease, and it's a lot easier to work through negative thoughts and emotions than it is to cure yourself of cancer, which is one of the most common ways negative emotions manifest in your body.

When I use the term "check in with yourself," I mean ask yourself some questions like—are my friends picking me up or dragging me down? Are my feelings and actions rooted in fear? This one is tricky because our egos do *not* like to admit FEAR. Am I attached to the outcome I expect? Do my actions align with my values?

I've heard many times we're the sum total of the five people closest to us. When I first heard this, I looked at my closest circle of friends and knew I had to make some serious adjustments. Energies are absolutely contagious. If you surround yourself with positive people, they can raise your vibration when you're feeling low and vice versa.

As I started to remove low vibrational people from my immediate world, the universe quickly filled that space with people who operate at a much higher frequency, which means *I* now operate at a much higher frequency. You should give it a good, honest try and see how much easier things start to fall into place in your life. It feels like magic, and it's available to every single one of us, but it does require a big step out of the all-too-familiar comfort zone. It's definitely tough to curtail or sever old friendships, even if they are toxic, but holding onto them is a sure way to slow or crush your progress toward inner peace. Then someone else's drama can become your brain tumor or inability to have a fulfilling life.

Checking in with yourself also means questioning your habits and hobbies. If you're watching low-vibrational content on the internet or TV, like the news or violent movies, these things will leave an imprint on you, whether you realize it or not. This leads to worrying about things that probably don't really exist in the first place. If you don't give negative things any attention or energy, they will cease to exist in your world, and you can fill that space with things that make you feel good, such as spending time in nature or finding an outlet for the creative energy we all have inside of us just waiting to be released. As you do this, you will begin tuning into a higher frequency and the universe will align you with higher vibrational prosperity, health, friends, and partners. Life will begin to flow in a rhythm that feels much better than when you are focused on what you *don't* have and what you don't want.

Worrying is literally creating more of that thing you don't want, by giving it your energy. This sends the message to the universe that you're operating on a lower frequency, and it will have a low vibrational response. This is the Universal Law of Attraction, and it can work greatly to your advantage if you have positive thoughts and get in tune with nature. I promise you! Like my friend and mentor Keith Leon—author of *Walking With My Angels* and many more amazing books—likes to say, "It only works 100% of the time!"

CHAPTER TEN

Start by changing your negative thought patterns

Equanimity is the harmony of mind, body, and soul. It is also a description of the best way to be "in flow," but it took me a long time and a lot of hard lessons to find anything resembling this type of composure. My path to inner peace, healing past traumas, and breaking old habits started because someone was kind enough to help me become aware of some basic truths, which is why I'm sharing this information with you—paying it forward, if you will.

Our lives would be much easier if they'd teach us this stuff in grade school, rather than prioritizing monetary advancement in the name of security. Would you rather have a million dollars to be able to pay someone to "treat" your cancer or have the ability to let your body "cure" itself from any disease that tries to enter your sphere? Because that's what your body is designed to do!

It's important to stay in shape mentally and physically before life throws you a curveball, because it's a lot easier to prevent a problem than to try to fix it after it rears its ugly head. The sooner you can find your equanimity, the sooner all of the lights will start turning green before you get to them and the smoother everything will flow for you. It only requires a minimal effort on your part to start noticing big results and, as you raise your vibration, it will be contagious to those around you, which they will then spread to everyone they come in contact with.

What are you waiting for? Consider this a gentle nudge from the universe to get curious, get out of your comfort zone, and explore what you're really capable of.

I've been guilty of ignoring the nudge from the universe plenty of times in my life, mostly through second-guessing or not listening to my intuition, and it's led me down some dark roads. The darkest of those roads came in the form of insomnia that lasted more than two years. When I suddenly lost the ability to sleep, I thought something must have changed in my brain chemistry, that somehow I had managed to break the "off" switch in my brain, and it was maddening! I hadn't had any recent major life changes, but I did have a lot of stress and emotions I had been suppressing for years with drugs and alcohol. It finally caught up to me in the form of crippling insomnia that began pouring into every facet of my life, and I felt helpless to solve the riddle.

When I told a friend I felt like I was dying slowly and how the frustration of not being able to sleep just added to my inability to sleep and the insomnia seemed to be feeding on itself, he suggested a book called *Mindfulness: Finding Peace In a Frantic World* by Mark Williams and Danny Penman. That book gently introduced me to meditation and the science behind it, which is when things started slowly getting better. I began meditating for ten to twenty minutes a day, or at least going through the motions, in hopes of an instant transformation. I started noticing a shift in how I was feeling, but meditation should be viewed as a practice, rather than a cure, and it does get easier with time.

At first, I felt like I was putting a lot of effort into doing nothing, which is the opposite of how we're programmed to believe we can be productive at anything! As I kept practicing, the voice in my head got quieter and my brain chatter began to slow down. The voice in my head had been very loud, distracting me with worries and concerns about things that hadn't even happened and probably never would.

Solving imaginary problems is a massive waste of time and energy, yet we do it most of the time we're awake. Overthinking is pervasive in most cultures, and it's a self-defense mechanism created by fear, instilled at a very early age. Fear of what "other people think" is a big one, stemming from our animalistic drive to want to fit in because we are social and status-seeking creatures who believe there is safety in numbers.

I'm often amused by folks who need to proclaim, "We're not sheeple," which implies they do not follow the herd or belong to any kind of group—real independent mavericks. Then they go back to their peers to get praise on their profound insight on what's wrong with the world and their bold stance of sovereignty. Now they have created two groups, sheeple and not sheeple, and this increases their social status with the not sheeple. Can you see the paradox here? Truly independent thinkers don't need to proclaim they are not sheeple, and the thought would never cross their minds.

The fear programming we receive growing up is pretty darn thorough. For example, we're taught to fear strangers, which can lead to a fear of travel, which can lead to a lifetime of looking at the world through a very narrow window. This primes you to believe the reports of world news from whatever source you consider trusted. News outlets, politicians, and religions sell fear because it's easy low-hanging fruit that helps them line their pockets with no regard for the effect it has on an entire society. Fear grabs our attention because of our instinct to stay safe, and that has been manipulated for thousands of years as a means to control the masses for someone else's, usually greedy, nefarious intentions.

If you follow the money and dig deep enough into all of your fears, you will end up at the feet of someone who profits from keeping you from knowing your full potential. They don't want you to know you don't need them or anyone else to have a fantastic life. I'm sure you've all heard President Franklin

D. Roosevelt's famous inauguration speech in which he says, "The only thing we have to fear is fear itself." He nailed it perfectly. The only thing holding us back from living up to our full potential is the belief we need to rely on someone else to keep us safe from the boogieman, when it's been the boogieman who was guiding you the whole time!

As most of you are aware, the big profits in the healthcare system come from treating illness rather than curing it, and the medical system seems to have a lot more treatments than cures. Good news! The miraculous human body can cure itself from 99% of all physical ailments. I stop at 99% because if your appendix bursts or you have a bone sticking out of your leg, you need the help of someone else to fix it. When we learn to get our pesky brain out of the way, the body will heal itself, and the same is true for the mind!

Recently, someone told me they've cured themselves of cancer three times, and it was pretty easy. Another friend and mentor of mine, Lisa Warner, cured herself of cancer and wrote a fantastic book that goes into more detail about how to do this, *The Simplicity of Self-Healing*, which I highly recommend. When we hear the same thing, over and over our whole lives, and see manufactured evidence of it being true, it's easy to believe the lies and buy into them. I've lost several friends and family members to cancer, and I wish I knew then what I know now.

Fear of death and what will happen after, if we don't believe the right thing or live a certain way, is another big issue. I think this one has caused more damage throughout history than any other single fear, and it causes people to dedicate their entire lives to preparing for the ideal afterlife, or at least avoiding burning in hell for eternity.

First of all, I'm a father, and I know that there is NOTHING my son could do that would make me want him to burn for eternity, regardless of what he believes. A loving God will not do that to you either! This is another case of someone telling you what to fear and then selling you the "magic shield" you need to protect yourself from a manufactured destiny. After all, isn't the salvation of your soul worth a few dollars a day? No, it's not, because your soul's destiny was planned long before you entered this body and it's going to be fine—way better than fine. I've studied a lot of near-death experiences, and every person tells the same story when they return from the grips of death. Not one of them is ever told they will be going to hell. In fact, it's quite the opposite, regardless of their religious background and beliefs, or lack of.

My mother is a devout Christian woman, and I grew up going to church and Sunday school regularly. Most of it didn't make any sense to me, even back then. It didn't feel right and true. Most of it still doesn't to this day. For example, if God only put Adam and Eve on this planet and incest is a sin, how did the rest of us get here? I'm no mathematician, but something here doesn't add up. Or why is my history teacher passing around 60-million-year-old dinosaur bones, if the Earth is really only a few thousand years old? Or how could God love me, but send me to hell for not following the rules? That doesn't sound like the unconditional love they are constantly promoting to me.

History class also taught me about how the "crusaders" and several other Christian-based religious powerhouses spread their message of "salvation and unconditional love" through manipulation first and, when that didn't work, they would start torturing and killing people until those remaining had a "sudden moment of clarity" and figured out how to fall in line and not get killed. Then, the people who had been "saved" had their complete history erased and replaced with the history their conquerors decided should be passed on to future generations.

The world we live in now, especially in the west, is a reflection of that kind of activity that's been going on for thousands of years, resulting in a very big, very misled congregation. Religions are on the decline, which means a lot of people have the same "doesn't ring right and true" feeling I do. The downside of this is that because we have been lied to by so many people throughout our lives about matters of spirituality and some of the other big mysteries we all ponder from one time or another, we have trouble deciphering the facts from the fiction. So much so, many of us close ourselves off to these concepts altogether, lessening the quality of life we would have if people would just stop lying to us about some very important things.

One of my favorite parables is about a Christian and a Hindu man walking and talking about religious matters. The Hindu man says, "I'm from India, and I've never heard of these things before today, so does this mean I'm going to burn in hell since I haven't devoted my life to worshiping and praising your God?"

The Christian man says, "Not if you didn't know about it."

The Hindu man asks, "Then why did you tell me?"

The truth is, there's no such thing as hell, except for the one you create with your own mind if you choose to do so. Remember, where your thoughts go, your energy flows! It took a long time for me to get that through my thick skull, but better late than never!

This is my last attempt to make this point as clear as possible. If you want to have a positive and fulfilling life, you MUST start by changing negative thought patterns. We've all done it way too much, but when you keep thinking, "Gee, I'd sure like to get out of the rut that I'm in," you're literally giving your energy to the very rut you are trying to escape, which keeps you there.

Instead, focus your thoughts on what you DO want to happen. Make yourself feel like you would if that thing had already happened, and you will get positive results! The more you practice, the faster it will happen. I've watched this work over and over in my own life and the lives of those around me.

We've all heard the term "misery loves company," and it's absolutely true. When someone is feeling negative, they instinctively try to get others to join them (Pack mentality rises again.). Don't let someone pull you into their sadness or anger, because negative energy can be contagious, too, even if you agree with their stance.

We love to blame others and choose sides, but the truth is it doesn't matter who the president is! There's no single person who is going to save the world and no magic bullet is going to make your life better. If you want to see positive change in the world around you, give more than you take, volunteer to help those in need, get a dog from your local animal shelter, and take it for a walk in nature. Help at a retirement home or a soup kitchen. The list of ways you can volunteer in your community is long. Getting involved will raise your vibration, and it will raise the vibration of the community around you!

If someone lashes out at you, they're projecting their inner turmoil onto anyone who will receive it—misery loves company. Instead of responding to anger with more anger—using resistance to combat resistance only creates more resistance—try using empathy and kindness. They are likely just confused and scared and probably need a hug more than anything else.

Ultimately, we only have each other, so if you have a neighbor or someone else you've been at odds with, take them some cookies and embrace your differences, which could easily become useful strengths for the challenges on the horizon. If we stand together with all of our differences and individual strengths supporting the collective, we will be unbreakable! COLLECTIVELY, we need to stop focusing on what's wrong with the world and start focusing on what's right. This has to start with raising your own vibration first. Then that energy becomes contagious to the people around you and creates a ripple effect that spreads farther than you can imagine. This is truly how one single person can change the world!

Before we came into this world, our souls let the universe know what our intentions were and what lessons we wanted to learn during this incarnation. That is called a "life plan." We're born with amnesia, and it's our life's task to learn the lessons we chose. Believe it or not, many of those lessons involve struggles and the growth that comes from them, which is why we're born with amnesia. If you knew what your life plan was, you'd avoid the struggle as much as possible and take the most direct path you could find toward accomplishing the intentions you conveyed to the universe, instead of having a real life, full of all the ups and downs and lessons that come from living authentically without taking shortcuts to get your lessons out of the way.

Start by changing your negative thought patterns

Once you begin to understand why you're actually here, deep healing will begin. Regardless of how you feel about your belongings, I can assure you your soul isn't gaining any wisdom from the things you own but rather from the things you do.

CHAPTER ELEVEN

Bridging the gap

It is paramount we spend as much time as possible communing with nature. Too many people believe we are separate from nature. That disconnect is very dangerous! It's dangerous to our overall well-being, and it causes great harm to our fragile yet resilient environment, which means it is threatening our very existence! In an effort to bridge this disconnect—and save the planet—I am starting a school that will get kids fully in tune with nature. The education provided will leave no doubt in their minds that we are all a part of nature, and we will teach them how to make the most of it.

I've decided to hold off on selling my rafting company and moving onto a sailboat for now. Instead, I'm going to use my Idaho Outfitters License to offer a five-day course that will be totally free the first year for kids who are fourteen to eighteen years old. The following year, it will be free for kids twelve to eighteen.

Because the local Shoshone tribe calls the Salmon River the "Medicine River"—I truly believe all rivers are medicine—I'm going to name the school "The Medicine River Academy."

The five days will be spent camping and floating on this amazing river in one of the most beautiful settings I've ever seen—and, as you may have noticed, I get around.

Cell phones don't work where we're going, so we will have the kids' undivided attention, and they will be more inclined to embrace the moment as we teach them First Aid and CPR on the first day. We will get them familiar with camping gear, and they will build and tear down their own camp every day. On day one, we will also teach them how to safely build and extinguish a fire using a fire pan and show them how to cook with a Dutch oven. They will prepare their own meals every day, with supervision, of course. We'll do yoga every day to get everyone stretched out and grounded before getting on the water.

I'm guessing most kids and their parents could really use some grounding and may have never even heard of it or know what a great tool it is—that we all have access to for free—for keeping a level head when unexpected circumstances arise, and they will arise. The same is true for meditation.

We will float to a new campsite each day, doing some swift water rescue and navigation training along the way. After we hit land, the kids will set up their camp, and we will introduce them to the magical healing powers of the plants that are all around us, all of the time, unless you live in the Sahara Desert or Antarctica. We're in the "high desert" here, and there's medicine growing all around us, just like there is where you live.

They should teach us in kindergarten which plants will make us sick and which ones will make us feel better. Mother Nature has provided everything we need to treat and cure our ailments. We just need to know what to look for. Where do you think pharmaceutical companies find their ingredients? Not on another planet, I can assure you of that. We will empower the youth with the knowledge that will allow them to eliminate the expensive middleman, including all of the misguided diagnoses from the so-called experts. That way, they can start to take their mental and physical health into their own hands with ease.

Every evening, we will have drum circles and get silly with different music specialists who come to assist, and everyone will participate. Artists will teach the kids how to nurture their creativity. We will do team-building exercises every day, and one of our stops will be at a place along the river that has a natural rock-climbing wall and a challenge course set up. It's going to be fantastic for the students and the instructors and will help raise the collective vibration!

By the time the kids leave, they should be able to teach their friends and families how to safely navigate rivers and be in tune with nature. Some of our students may eventually choose to become raft guides, and all of our students will fall in love with nature—and we always protect the things we love!

With that, I will say goodbye for now. I hope you've had as much fun reading as I have had reliving these stories. In fact, I had so much fun writing this, I plan to start on another book soon. I still have a bunch of fun stuff to share, with new adventures being created all of the time. There are some references to other resources in the back of this book and contact information for the river academy in case you would like to donate or participate in some way. Remember to always be kind and respect each other, and when the universe nudges you to leave your comfort zone, Don't Fight It, Just Ride It!

About the Author

Matt Rigsby is the founder and president of The Medicine River Academy, a school dedicated to empowering youth to navigate rivers and be fully in tune with Mother Earth.

When he's not on the river, Matt enjoys mountain biking, skiing, sailing, kite surfing, long walks in nature, writing, and spending time with his wife Adrienne and their pets. They are all soon to be sailing around the world!

As a new author, he hopes sharing his stories in a humorous and vulnerable way will be a source of inspiration to people on their quest for self-discovery, joy, and a life that is fulfilling in every way.

Rowing the Salmon River with Charlotte

If you're interested in contributing to The Medicine River Academy, you can go to www.medicineriver.org or call (208) 756-7805.

If you want to go rafting with us, you can go to www.salmonriverrecreation.com or call (208) 756-4386.

www.ingramcontent.com/pod-product-compliance
Lightning Source LLC
LaVergne TN
LVHW051849080426
835512LV00018B/3152